COUNTRY · EXPLORERS ·

A Visit to

CUBA

By Rebecca Phillips-Bartlett

BEARPORT
PUBLISHING

Minneapolis, Minnesota

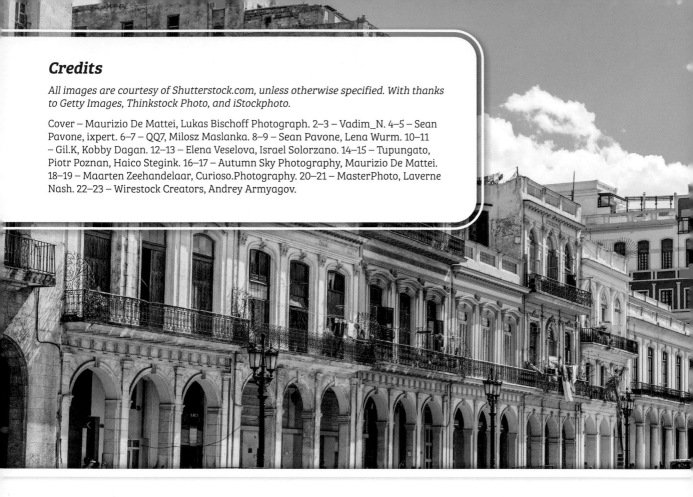

Credits

All images are courtesy of Shutterstock.com, unless otherwise specified. With thanks to Getty Images, Thinkstock Photo, and iStockphoto.

Cover – Maurizio De Mattei, Lukas Bischoff Photograph. 2–3 – Vadim_N. 4–5 – Sean Pavone, ixpert. 6–7 – QQ7, Milosz Maslanka. 8–9 – Sean Pavone, Lena Wurm. 10–11 – Gil.K, Kobby Dagan. 12–13 – Elena Veselova, Israel Solorzano. 14–15 – Tupungato, Piotr Poznan, Haico Stegink. 16–17 – Autumn Sky Photography, Maurizio De Mattei. 18–19 – Maarten Zeehandelaar, Curioso.Photography. 20–21 – MasterPhoto, Laverne Nash. 22–23 – Wirestock Creators, Andrey Armyagov.

Library of Congress Cataloging-in-Publication Data is available at www.loc.gov or upon request from the publisher.

ISBN: 979-8-88509-969-1 (hardcover)
ISBN: 979-8-88822-148-8 (paperback)
ISBN: 979-8-88822-289-8 (ebook)

© 2024 BookLife Publishing
This edition is published by arrangement with BookLife Publishing.

For more information, write to Bearport Publishing, 5357 Penn Avenue South, Minneapolis, MN 55419.

CONTENTS

COUNTRY TO COUNTRY

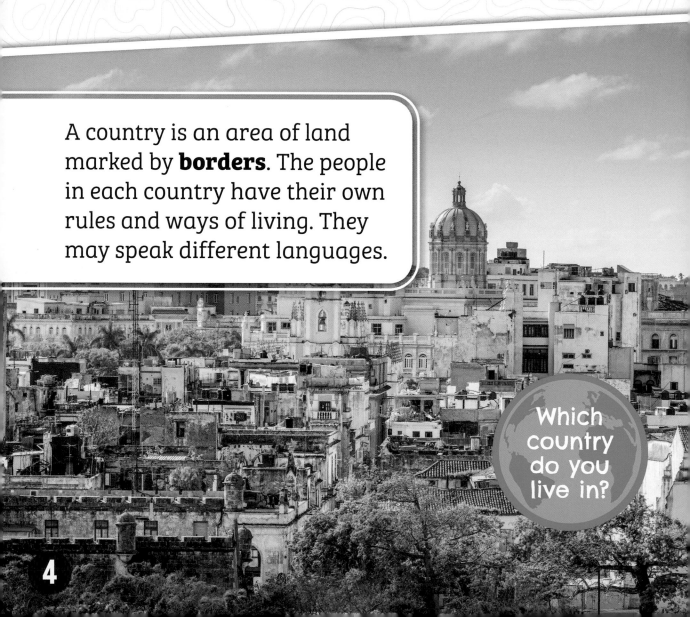

A country is an area of land marked by **borders**. The people in each country have their own rules and ways of living. They may speak different languages.

Which country do you live in?

Each country around the world has its own interesting things to see and do. Let's take a trip to visit a country and learn more!

Have you ever visited another country?

TODAY'S TRIP IS TO
CUBA!

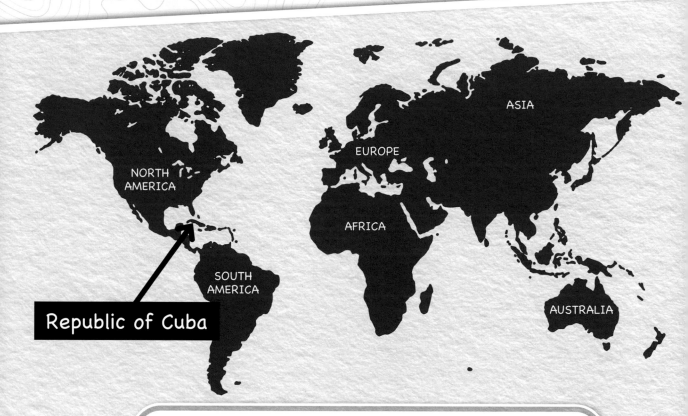

ASIA

EUROPE

NORTH
AMERICA

AFRICA

Republic of Cuba

SOUTH
AMERICA

AUSTRALIA

The Republic of Cuba is an island nation in the Caribbean Sea. This country is part of the **continent** of North America.

FACT FILE

Capital city: Havana
Main language: Spanish
Currency: Cuban peso
Flag:

Currency is the type of money that is used in a country.

HAVANA

We'll start our trip in Havana, the capital city of Cuba. Havana is the largest city in Cuba. It has many beaches and buildings.

Museum of the Revolution, Havana

Havana has more than 50 museums. They are about many different things. We can even visit a museum all about playing cards!

9

MUSIC AND DANCE

In Havana, there are often bands playing in the streets.

Let's listen to some music! Cuban music often tells stories about the country's history. A popular kind of music is called Son Cubano. It is based on music from Spain and Africa.

Cuba also has lots of dances, such as the rumba and the mambo. The country's **national** music and dance is called Danzón.

Rumba dancers in Havana

FOOD

Lots of meals in Cuba come with rice, beans, and plantains.

Feeling hungry? Let's eat one of Cuba's national dishes. Ropa vieja is a beef dish served with rice and beans.

We could also try Cuba's national fruit. It is a kind of berry called mamey sapote. On the island, it is often used in smoothies or ice cream.

Mamey sapotes

NATURE

Next, we'll head into nature. Cuba has beaches, **jungles**, and forests. There, we might spot Cuba's national tree, the royal palm. These trees can grow more than 65 feet (20 m) tall.

Cuba's forests are home to many amazing animals, such as the bee hummingbird. This is the world's smallest bird. Bee hummingbirds grow to be only about 2 inches (6 cm) long!

Some of the world's smallest frogs live here, too.

FORTRESS IN SANTIAGO DE CUBA

The city of Santiago de Cuba is home to a **fortress** called Castillo de San Pedro de la Roca. The building looks like a castle, but no one lives there.

People looking out from the fortress can see the Caribbean Sea.

Castillo de San Pedro de la Roca was built on cliffs to keep **pirates** away. Today, there is a museum about pirates inside the fortress.

BASEBALL

Baseball is one of the most popular sports in Cuba. Many people play it in the streets.

Baseball was brought to the country by a young Cuban who went to study in the United States. When he came home, the student took a bat and ball to teach people how to play.

Havana has the world's second-largest baseball stadium.

LATINOAMERICANO

CAYO LARGO DEL SUR

Cayo Largo is known for its white, sandy beaches.

The country of Cuba is made of many islands. Cuba is the name of the biggest island. One of the many little islands is called Cayo Largo del Sur.

Cayo Largo del Sur is home to the Sea Turtle Rescue Center. Every year, hundreds of sea turtles lay their eggs on the island's beaches. When the eggs **hatch**, workers at the center help look after the baby turtles.

BEFORE YOU GO

We can't forget to visit Fusterlandia. In this part of Havana, the buildings and streets are covered in colorful **mosaics**.

We could also visit caves. Some caves in Cuba are full of water, so we can swim in them. The deepest cave is called Giant's Eye.

What have you learned about Cuba on this trip?

GLOSSARY

borders lines that show where one place ends and another begins

continent one of the world's seven large land masses

fortress a strong building from which people can defend an area

hatch to break out of an egg

jungles thick forests in hot places

mosaics patterns or pictures made from small pieces of colorful stone or glass

national having to do with a country

pirates people who attack and rob ships at sea

INDEX